#stronger

Courtney Allison Brown

Somebody's Answer LLC

"Be somebody's answer today..."

Published & Printed in the United States of America

First Edition

ISBN: 978-0692291146

Somebody's Answer LLC

www.somebodysanswer.org

For the walking wounded…may your

broken-heart be mended, your life be made

whole, and your joy restored…

You are NOT alone.

Get #stronger

Opening Thoughts...

Life's journey is certainly not for the faint of heart. In order to meander through the vast complexities that meet us from day to day, we must have faithful and persistent tenacity mixed with undying hope. It is that ferocious desire burning within us that keeps the flames of our passion for purpose ignited from moment to moment.

To keep your dream alive is not the difficulty. To yield to the giving-and-receiving tug of war in love, is not particularly hard either. To work for an assumed cause, or the greater good's noble gesture is payment in full. However, frustration exists in the realization that life does not always render us the most ideal circumstances to support a continuous flow of blessings. Our good times are often marked with the tests, trials, pain and disappointment often associated with unfulfilled expectations.

May I ask you a question? What derailed you? What pulled your attention away from purposeful passion to linger in this place?

This is not the place of your intended destination. There is so much more for you. Right now, however, you must grow. It is needful that you evolve here so rest, but do not become comfortable for there is yet more!

If you believe there is more for you, take my hand and enter this journey with me to life, to joy, and to the true healing that your soul needs. Each day, for the next eight days, I want you to devote a specific time to interacting fully with this text. Dive in with an open heart and respond fully to the questions that appear at the end of each encouraging and thought provoking sentiment. Some days you'll laugh. Other days may bring tears. But, everyday will foster deep and meaningful change. Let's get *#stronger* together.

Day 1: Keeping it 100

One of the most overused colloquialisms in recent times is "keeping it 100." It speaks to being honest, true and authentic. There is an unspoken, but mutually understood respect and value in being real. Being real speaks to being fully you, fully aware, and fully unique in your opinions, responses and perceptions of the reality that you live in.

For the next eight days of our time together, be open and transparent about your feelings and experiences. The only way to truly grow is to fully acknowledge all portions of your daily evolution whether your perceptions of them are good or bad. From the onset and throughout this interactive journey, it is incumbent upon you to take full responsibility for your involvement in your own life's attractions, decisions, desires, passions, histories, beliefs and perceptions. What others see upon meeting you is merely a surface level presentation of what lies within your soul. Furthermore, how you perceive others is much more than what meets your eyes. How you experience them is an intricate interweaving of commonality, attractions, and awareness of all that you've already encountered in your life.

The way in which you engage people and opportunities presents an awesome opportunity for truth and acknowledgment. In other words, much of what has happened to you is the direct result of your own decision-making. The first person you must acknowledge responsibility to is yourself. Ask yourself, what part did I play in my financial difficulty? Did I save or spend beyond what I could afford? Your issue may be your health. There are certainly genetic pre-dispositions to things that none of us have any control over. However, ask yourself if you've really given yourself fully to the part you can have influence over. Have you eaten right and exercised, or have you allowed the pressures or pleasures of life, along with a lack of discipline, keep you from healthy meals and an active lifestyle? Your dreams may not have been realized as of yet. But, have you stopped going after what brings you joy to going through the motions? Have you ceased to live and allowed your moments to yield to existing? Even more, within your inner circle of friends and relationships, are you attracting the same sorts of experiences?

Many of us blame God, the world, and our network of associations for working against us. A closer look might reveal that if we "keep it 100" we have been just as responsible if not more for our negative outcomes as those experiences and people to whom we have blamed our unfavorable outcomes on.

Here lies our first chance in our time together to get **#stronger**. Identify at least one experience,

disappointment, or relationship that has recently given you pause. Fully address its intricacies and nuances in a way that you haven't before. In this moment, shift your perception from *"I can't believe that this happened to me"* to *"I believe that this is working for me."*

#stronger Action Steps:

(1) Below, write out the experience. (2) Then, write out your responses to that experience and how it affected you. (3) Evaluate your responsibility in that experience. (4) Finally, write out a purposeful action step. Ask yourself, what can I do to get **#stronger?**

_____

_____

_____

_____

_____

_____

_____

_____

_____

_____

_____

_____

_____

_____

_____

_____

_____

_____

_____

_____

_____   Romans 8:28

Day 2: Am I enough?

What a familiar question. Each of us at some point through failures, frailties, foibles, tragedies and triumphs have asked ourselves, am I enough? Did I do enough? Did I love enough? Did I give enough?

Am... I... enough?

Unfortunately, life and its winding turns sometimes causes us to view things from a problem-centered framework. We ask questions about our worthiness in order to isolate what's wrong, and to hopefully make changes. In general, it is not a bad practice to want to improve the self. For sure, to honestly view one's self in light of a more favorable improvement or standard is a great thing! However, when that process consistently turns into one of self-blaming, self-injury can result. If not careful, the very thing we believe is being inflicted upon us by another could turn into something that we subconsciously inflict upon ourselves.

Our joy then, towards experiencing a new situation, very easily gets swallowed in fear because we secretly wonder if what is good will become what's familiar particularly when what is familiar is painful. Haven't you said things like: *"this always happens to me, I'm used to it now"* or *"every time I let go, I get hurt,"* or my personal favorite, *"what's wrong with me?"*

The truth is, there is something wrong with all of us. We are human, flawed, fallible, and in all things capable of error. None of us is perfect no matter how incessantly we try to be. We will make mistakes. We will not handle every situation with the precision of an expert. We will not succeed at everything we attempt 100% of the time. Some goals won't be reached right away. Some relationships won't work out. **BUT**, the great thing is, there are some infallibles that we can rely on to navigate through the times when we question worthiness, and give way to the temptation to fear success.

We are **unique**ly crafted by the hand of a loving God. He does not make mistakes. You are who you are down to the very essence of your thoughts, your deepest emotions, your ambitions and inhibitions. Everything about you is matchlessly, indescribably you. Amongst people, there are similarities in abilities, ideas and thoughts; but you are the only one who does what you do like you do! Can you accept that today? Don't go another moment feeling insignificant because the God of the universe's worlds made you so special, that not another

anywhere has your fingerprint.

The irony of being humanly flawed does not make

you less **valuable**. When we encounter circumstances

which make us feel devalued, we tend to question our

significance. It is a natural response. However, the

rejections that we experience, the disappointments that we

feel, the disillusionment that looms before us at times, all

work for us. Let me explain. Instead of viewing your

challenges as confirmation to feelings of self-doubt, see

them as the resistance that you need to build muscles of

faith in yourself! Those challenges were never meant to

destroy you. They were intended to show you how

valuable, how "enough" you really are.

Look at you! You were able to come through everything that you've been through and still be **alive**. As long as you're alive, there's opportunity to discover and operate in your best self's greatness. The world around you awaits the **unique**, **valuable**, **living** wonder called _____ (insert your name).

You are enough in every way and when you truly believe this, you will attract to you circumstances which confirm this truth or challenge you to become greater.

#stronger Action Steps:

(1) Without any hesitation, list the things that are unique to your truest self. (2) What are your greatest qualities? (3) What things do you consider flaws? (4) Now see yourself as the **unique, valuable, living** wonder that you are. What

is one way you can shape your perception to see yourself

as enough today?

_____

_____

_____

_____

_____

_____

_____

_____

_____

_____

_____

_____

_____

_____

_____

_____

_____

_____

_____

_____

_____

_____

_____

_____Psalm 139:14

Day 3: Love Yourself

In order to love others, one must first functionally love one's self. Oddly enough, this tends to be no small feat. It comes naturally to many of us to extend ourselves in empathetic compassion to our families and loved ones. However, it seems to be really hard for many of us to extend that same love to ourselves. Newsflash: Loving others is a healthy overflow of first loving the self.

For me, I had deficits in this area because I was concerned that loving myself would make me appear selfish. So, being superwoman for everyone else often at the expense of my own well-being became the norm for years. Within my family, with my friends and even in romantic relationships, I was reputed as the reliable one. I was the person that everybody could count on to be everything that was needed whenever it was needed. I would give until it hurt and often feel depleted because I was not receiving to the capacity that I was giving. For years, I complained about not having someone to give to me until I realized a phenomenally simple truth. Giving to myself, being patient with myself, encouraging myself, believing in myself, forgiving myself, while loving myself -at least as much as I'd freely disbursed these gifts to others -would make me a truly loving person.

Think about it, are you preferring others so much that you never prefer yourself?

I encourage you to spend some time really loving you! Discover your likes and dislikes. Enjoy your time alone. Render to yourself the understanding that you keep expecting others to give you. Sacrifice to accomplish your dreams at least as much as you sacrifice to help others accomplish theirs. In so doing, you will teach others how to treat you by first treating yourself like the wonderful person that you are. In the long and short run, you'll find that a sincere appreciation of all that you are created to be is very attractive. Particular people, places, and things will enter your path. Your ability to fully love others will be enhanced because you first loved all of you.

#stronger Action Steps:

(1) Make a list of things that you enjoy. (2) Choose one thing from the list that you can do today and then do it. (3) Report how it made you feel. (4) Each day, commit to doing at least one thing from your list.

_____

_____

_____

_____

_____

_____

_____

_____

_____

_____

_____

_____

_____Matthew 19:19

Day 4: The Other Brother...Lost in the House

There is a very familiar story told of a prodigal son. He decided to ask for his inheritance and to leave home to find his way in the world. He had an awesome time for a season living in the fast lane with his riches and friends. Eventually, his money ran out along with his friends and his good times. He found himself in the hog pen in shame. As the story would have it, the young man returned home and received the love of a compassionate father who killed a fatted calf for him in celebration of his return. (adapted from Luke 15:11-32)

Everybody was extremely happy and enjoying the party except one person-the other brother. Here was the older brother who'd stayed and served his father. Here was the brother who'd not blown his inheritance on riotous living. Yet, it seemed as if he were invisible. Where was his celebration for being honorable, loyal and true? There was none.

I can almost hear that angry brother saying, "*I've been obedient and done all you've asked me to do but you never celebrate me. I didn't take your money and waste it Daddy. I've served you well…Daddy, do you even see me? Do I matter to you at all? Am I important to you?*"

According to the Scriptures, when the other, older brother expresses his frustration and disappointment, the father tells him: "My son, you are always with me, and everything I have is yours. But we had to celebrate and be glad, because this brother of yours was dead and is alive again; he was lost and is found" (Luke 15:31-32 NIV). This is a fantastic depiction of the mercy of God towards the prodigal son; but can you imagine how the other brother- whom we never focus on in this text- felt?

Have you ever felt insignificant?

Our society is so problem-centered that we sometimes forget to spend adequate time appreciating those people who are faithful, dedicated and full of integrity. If you watch the news for any length of time you'll find more attention paid to things that are wrong than to things that are right. Walk into your average classroom and you may just find more time given to the children who are misbehaving than to the children who consistently obey and strive for success. With your own children, how much time do you really spend praising their strengths compared to magnifying their weaknesses?

Certainly, the other brother should not have let his frustration mount to bitterness and latent jealousy; but if you really look into the dynamics of his experience from his perspective, I'm sure you can understand.

Just in case no one has told you recently, you are amazing and phenomenal. You are significant and you do matter. Your brilliance is not minimized because it is not always acknowledged. There are times when you may crave reassurance and encouragement. There may even be times in your environment where you believe too much time is being given to someone or something that is producing a problem. Know this, what you've sown in compassion, truthfulness, loyalty, faithfulness and sacrifice has not gone unnoticed. You will reap even if your harvest does not spring forth from the same place in which you planted it!

Without a doubt, we could all stand to recognize the

people in our lives that we most ignore because everybody

deserves to know and to hear how important they are.

However, if you never receive this validation from a

human source, know that you are important to God. He

sees you. You are in no way invisible to Him. He knows

right where you are and nothing that you have given to

others has gone beyond his watchful eye.

#stronger Action Steps:

(1) In the space provided below, write a letter to yourself. In it, tell yourself how much you are appreciated and loved. Take the time to describe how significant you are in the many roles that you play (i.e. mother, husband, father, wife, friend). (2) Whenever you are feeling overlooked, read this letter. Get *#stronger.*

_____

_____

_____

_____

_____

_____

_____

_____

_____

_____

_____

_____

_____

_____

_____

_____

_____

_____

_____Luke 12:7

Day 5: Letting Go

One of the hardest things in the world to do is to let go.

I can remember when BJ, my son, was a baby and he needed me for everything. Soon, he started to walk and didn't want to be held so much anymore because it was time for him to discover the world. Not too long after that came school, and teachers, and friends. I woke up the other day and that same little boy was now tall enough to look me in the eye and to enter high school. My, how time flies!

What BJ needed from me when he was a baby is definitely not what he needs from me as a teenager. Should I determine that I want to provide for him on the level that I did when he was two years old, our relationship, would be completely dysfunctional. Because he is maturing, I must also mature and evolve to make accommodations. Part of that process is letting go and it's not easy at all.

This year was the first year in almost five years that BJ has not been with me on the ride to school or for the return home. On the weekends now, he has plans with his friends and activities for school to attend. In the past, we would have hung out together. But, I have to slowly let go. To hold on too tightly to my son would stunt his growth and mine.

The above is a simple example of my developing crisis of change; but it is not the only one. I have at times struggled in my friendships and intimate relationships to release a framework that has served its purpose. Do you identify?

Many times I've known that it was time to evolve, to change, to move away from or to totally cut off a person, an experience or a mode of thought; but, I just couldn't seem to take the necessary steps to do so. In those seasons of my life I have endured immense pain and heartache because I carried with me weight that was meant to be released. Sometimes what you're supposed to receive is delayed because you are holding onto an old framework. In other words, what is **new** cannot become evident until what is *old* is released.

It may not be a person, an experience, or a mode of thought. You may be housing negative emotions. Are you holding onto pain, unforgiveness, bitterness, frustration or

other destructive emotions? If so, you have to let them go.
In order to be healthy and whole, you must release those
things that plague and trouble you in order to make room
for more! Day by day, moment by moment, you must
reframe your thinking, your speech and your actions to
reflect the changes that you are making. At first, it may
hurt considerably. You may weep bitter tears if you have
to walk away from a friendship or relationship that no
longer serves you, or you it. But, if you can manage to
take steps to let go, to evolve, to change, to enter the next
phase of your journey, you will find that eventually you
will begin to heal and to enjoy the next chapter of your
life. There is more to your story. Letting go is only the
beginning of renewed joy, increased focus, and greater
strength!

#stronger Action Steps:

Consider your life as it is right now. What is currently causing you to be stagnant and immobilized? (1) Describe the experience, person, or emotion that is causing you to neglect forward progression. (2) Write an affirmative statement that you can easily remember when the temptation to neglect change occurs. (i.e. *The benefits of this change in my life far outweigh the current discomfort.*)

_____

_____

_____

_____

_____

_____

_____

_____

_____

_____

_____

_____

_____

_____

_____

_____

_____

_____

_____

_____Phillipians 3:13

Day 6: Losing vs. Gaining...

Death to anything – a marriage, a life, a dream, a friendship, a business – brings great loss and many times great sorrow. It would be inhumane and insensitive to pretend that the detachment that we experience when someone or something is removed from our lives is anything less than painful. We grieve in stages and sometimes fixate at certain places that our emotions will not allow us safe passage through. Other times we find ourselves spiraling through denial, anger, bargaining, and depression without true genuine acceptance of the process that we have found ourselves in.

Have you ever experienced the evolution of a relationship that felt like death and caused you to grieve? I have, many times. Certainly sometimes that "loss" was much more painful than other times. Like many of you, I

denied the presence of said "loss" until change slapped me

hard enough to consider that things were different now.

Things being different made me so very angry! I am a

creature of persistent consistency. How was I to accept the

fact that my attentions and affections had to be redirected?

How was I not to expect a call at a certain time or a usual

response to a stimulus that was slowly fading into no

more? Is this microphone on? Do you feel me at all?

The anger proposed by change caused me to bargain

and question. All the usual questions were asked. What

could I have done differently? Why was I not enough?

Don't you love me at all? Don't you care? My questions

turned from deeply personal to more deal making where I

sought to satiate my pain with comfortable, familiar

semblances of past connectedness.   This included boundary setting and lessening the level of intensity of a relationship. Unfortunately, all of this led to nothing but more pain and depression.

Have you ever been so depressed that you couldn't cry …couldn't sleep...couldn't eat?   Has the hurt ever radiated so deeply that certain clothes, certain memories, certain smells, particular places ripped you to the core of your wounded soul?   You're not alone. I've been there before and it wasn't cute at all. Without sleep and food you start getting delirious and irrational.   Lord, I'll spare you my meandering thoughts during that season of my life along with the accompanying uncharacteristic behavior.

But then, there comes a point, a pivotal point, when you begin to heal. And, you know what?   You probably won't even realize that it's happened until it does. One day, probably at a point when your attention is on

something unrelated, you'll find that you've started to

accept where you are as reality. You'll be able to forgive

genuinely and deeply. At some point, you'll see that what

seemed like the worst "loss" of your life was actually an

exponential gain!

Before you freak out and think I've lost my entire

mind and am still stuck in denial, stay with me.   If you're

reading this, I am positive that you've experienced varying

degrees of "death" or "loss." But, if you look back over

those situations, you'll see how much *#stronger* you

became.

Come with me to the place where a love one died.

Come with me to the place where you buried your dream.

Come, come now to the place where the love relationship

of your life dissipated into thin air.

Come with me, take my hand, and let's go to the place

where a friend became an enemy.

Come with me to the emotional jail cell you've been in

since the ink dried on your divorce papers.

Are you there with me? I acknowledge your hurt and the pain that plagues your soul from day to day. However, I want you to know that from where I stand my friend, you are not the same person today that you were when those things happened. You are indeed **#stronger**. You gained wisdom that you didn't have before. You are much more aware and astute. You have learned how to genuinely forgive. Forgiveness is truly the gift that keeps on giving.

Without it, hearts grow cold and bitter. How amazing that

yours stayed soft and pliable through all that you've

endured!

#stronger Action Steps:

(1) Below, identify and evaluate at least one thing that

seemed like a "loss" to you. (2) Then, take some time to

write out what lessons you learned and the ways in which

you grew because of it.

_____

_____

_____

_____

_____

_____

_____

_____

_____

_____

_____

_____

_____

_____

_____

_____

_____ Matthew 18:21

Day 7: Addicted to Pain...

Do you have a wound that won't heal or a pain that won't subside? It has seemed that just as you are making head way, something else occurs to wound you in the same spot again. I apologize ahead of time if this seems harsh...please forgive me. "Don't be addicted to pain." There's so much good in your life! Why would you waste time and energy on experiences that warrant you frustration repeatedly?

Listen, this is just between us, I promise. Be honest... Haven't you gone through this enough? Haven't you been hurt enough? Haven't you been disappointed enough? Get in the mirror and ask yourself, "how many times am I going to put myself in this position? How many times will I break my own heart?"

You are an amazing person with a wealth of talent and experiential grace. Don't squander this moment by losing focus now. Don't falter now. You've come too far to sabotage years of growth for a moment of familiarity.

Yes, for many of us, pain is familiar. We have subconsciously learned to accommodate and to adjust to pain so much that it is difficult to function where there is no drama. Unfortunately, we have become so accustomed to the bad behavior of ourselves and others that we excuse it by making room in our lives for it over and over again. We accept pain as normal and enter a continual cycle of hurting and complaining because of its existence.

This is to say that if a relationship has been in some way detrimental to your forward progression, why continue to invite it into your life although you are aware of its toxicity? If your health is in question, why would

you eat unhealthily, avoid exercise, and then suffer the

pain of illness? If you have a dream which has been

unrealized, why would you sabotage its realization with

both *intentional* and *unintentional* impediments?

You can live without the torturous familiarity of

pain. Life doesn't have to hurt for life to be recognizable

to you. In no way am I saying that life will be void of

painful experiences because that would be erroneous.

What I am saying is, it is possible to live peacefully

through the discomfort of the unknown. You can relieve

yourself of the toxicity which plagues you, and experience

life without holding on to what you think you cannot live

without.

#stronger Action Steps:

Below, answer the following questions: (1) What pain do you continuously allow in your life? (2) What cycle of pain continuously plagues you? (3) Now identify at least one action you can take in order to walk into freedom.

_____

_____

_____

_____

_____

_____

_____

_____

_____

_____

_____

_____

_____

_____

_____

_____

_____

_____

_____

_____

_____

_____Ecclesiastes 3:3

Day 8: Don't Let "It" Change You

Well, here we are at the end of our journey together. Just wanted to encourage you. Don't let the challenge that you're encountering change you. If you're kind, be kind. If you're wonderful, be wonderful. If you're loving, be loving. If you're compassionate, continue to be compassionate.

When you're hurting, it's easy to become vindictive and to lash out. However, hurt, pain, frustration or unforgiveness does not excuse bad behavior. Do the right thing even when the wrong thing is easy. Give till it hurts. Be genuine and sincere even in the face of ambiguity. And by all means don't change who you are just because your crisis is difficult. Love more!!! You'll feel better if you do. Trust me.

Negativity breeds negativity and is a Petri dish for bitterness, unforgiveness, mistrust, cynicism and more dysfunctional playmates. The more we operate in these states of being, the more we will attract experiences that confirm them. We end up joining the ranks of the walking wounded and we suffer in silence until challenges cause us to reveal our weaknesses. Some have left marriages because of pain only to encounter the same issues in another relationship. Some have left churches because they were disgusted with the leadership only to find that a new church had similar problems. Some have walked away from jobs because they didn't feel appreciated only to find that a new job was not much different. The common denominator in each situation is you. When you make changes, what you attract will change.

#stronger Action Steps:

Life is calling you higher my friend. Whatever impediments have caused you to stumble or to stagnate must cease to block your path. (1) So, as a last assignment, take a few moments to write out the desires of your heart. (2) What is your vision for your spirit, for your health, for your career & finances, and for your relationships? (3) Write out at least two specific action steps that you can take today to cause your vision to come to pass. It's up to you to get *#stronger* **!!!**

_____

_____

_____

_____

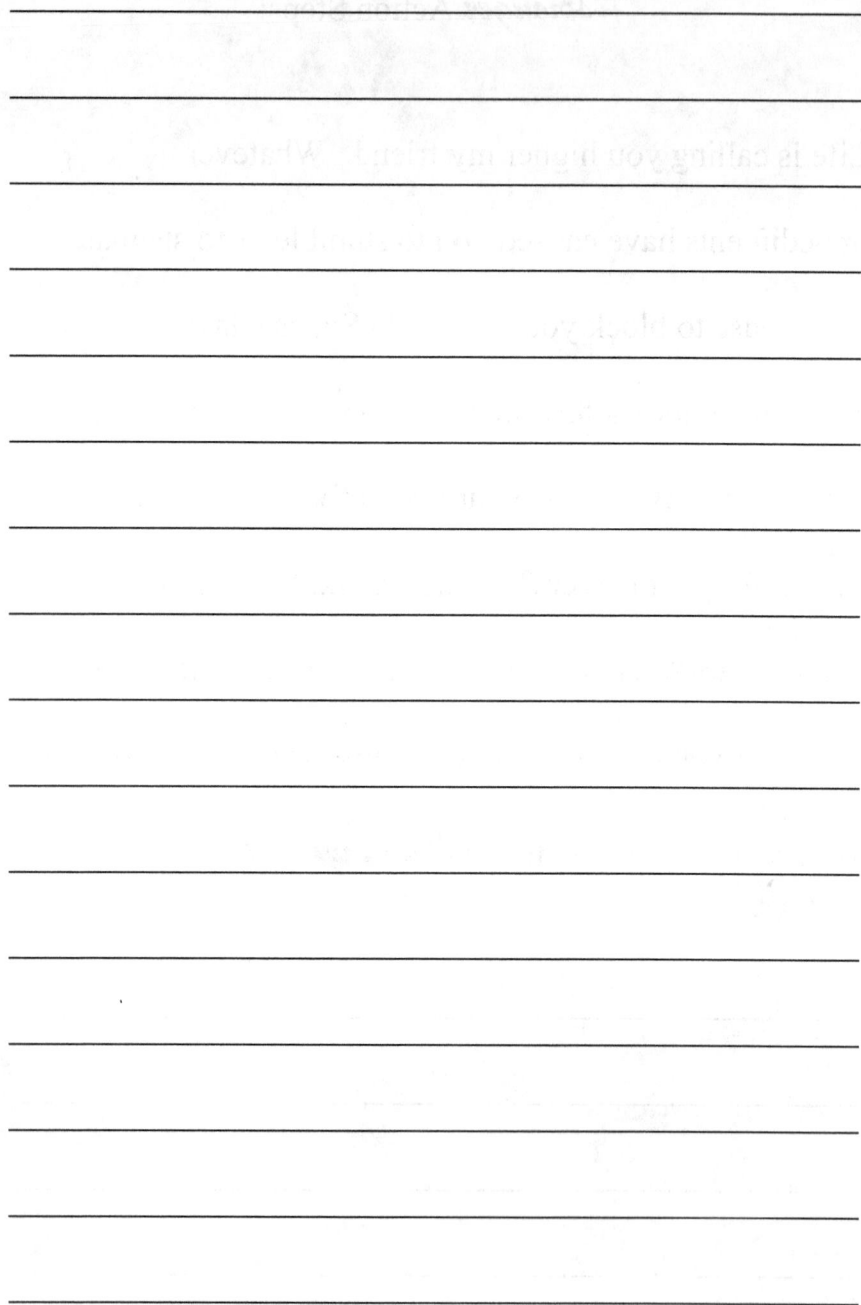

_____

_____

_____

_____

_____

_____

_____

_____

_____

_____

_____

_____

_____

_____Habakuk 2:2

A final word...

Perspective is everything. Choose today to see your experiences through the lens of growth and change. Choose today to...

Get #stronger!!!

To render your comments to the author, please send an email to somebodysanwer@gmail.com.

Thank you for your continued support.

www.ingramcontent.com/pod-product-compliance
Lightning Source LLC
Chambersburg PA
CBHW060616030426
42337CB00018B/3076